The INSIDE GUIDE

EARLY AMERICAN HISTORY

Native Americans in Early America

By Bert Wilberforce

Cavendish Square

Published in 2024 by Cavendish Square Publishing, LLC
2544 Clinton Street Buffalo, NY 14224

Website: cavendishsq.com

This publication represents the opinions and views of the author based on their personal experience, knowledge, and research. The information in this book serves as a general guide only. The author and publisher have used their best efforts in preparing this book and disclaim liability rising directly or indirectly from the use and application of this book.

Disclaimer: Portions of this work were originally authored by Mark Harasymiw and Thérèse Harasymiw and published as *Native Americans in Early America* (The Story of America). All new material this edition authored by Bert Wilberforce..

All websites were available and accurate when this book was sent to press.

Library of Congress Cataloging-in-Publication Data

Names: Wilberforce, Bert, author.
Title: Native Americans in early America / Bert Wilberforce.
Description: Buffalo, New York : Cavendish Square Publishing, [2024]. |
Series: Inside guide: early american history | Includes index.
Identifiers: LCCN 2022053034 (print) | LCCN 2022053035 (ebook) | ISBN
9781502667755 (library binding) | ISBN 9781502667748 (paperback) | ISBN
9781502667762 (ebook)
Subjects: LCSH: Indians of North America–History–Juvenile literature.
Classification: LCC E77.4 .W54 2024 (print) | LCC E77.4 (ebook) | DDC
973.1–dc23/eng/20221214
LC record available at https://lccn.loc.gov/2022053034
LC ebook record available at https://lccn.loc.gov/2022053035

Editor: Therese Shea
Designer: Deanna Paternostro

The photographs in this book are used by permission and through the courtesy of: Cover Everett Collection/Shutterstock.com; p. 4 Myrhonon/Wikimedia Commons; p. 6 Paul Henry Beaumont/Shutterstock.com; p. 7 Rainer Lesniewski/Shutterstock.com; p. 8 Robfergusonjr/Wikimedia Commons; p. 9 Scewing/Wikimedia Commons; p. 10 File Upload Bot (Kaldari)/Wikimedia Commons; pp. 12 (main), 21 RL65/Wikimedia Commons; p. 12 (inset) MatGTAM/Wikimedia Commons; p. 13 Dsdugan/Wikimedia Commons; p. 15 Junkyardsparkle/Wikimedia Commons; pp. 16, 18, 22 Courtesy of the Library of Congress; p. 19 Andrea Izzotti/Shutterstock.com; p. 20 Materialscientist/Wikimedia Commons; p. 24 (main) Morphart Creation/Shutterstock.com; p. 24 (inset) Artanisen/Wikimedia Commons; p. 26 Hohum/Wikimedia Commons; p. 27 (main) Jacob Boomsma/Shutterstock.com; p. 27 (inset) ThunderBirdEye/Shutterstock.com; p. 29 (left) Florn88/Wikimedia Commons; p. 29 (right) MarshalN20/Wikimedia Commons.

Some of the images in this book illustrate individuals who are models. The depictions do not imply actual situations or events.

CPSIA compliance information: Batch #CSCSQ24: For further information contact Cavendish Square Publishing LLC at 1-877-980-4450.

Printed in the United States of America

Find us on

CONTENTS

This is a map showing the cultural areas into which early Native American peoples are sometimes grouped. However, similarities between groups occurred across these imagined borders and differences occurred within them.

Arctic

Subarctic

Northwest Coast

Plateau

Great Basin

Plains

Northeast

California

Southwest

Southeast

Caribbe

Mesoamerica

Chapter One

IN THE EAST

The **Indigenous** peoples of North America settled in different environments all over the land that would later become the United States. Each culture that developed was rich with understanding of nature and complex in traditions. Those who study early Native Americans sometimes talk about them in terms of cultural areas. Peoples who lived in these regions shared certain cultural traits.

Northeast Cultures

The Northeast cultural area included today's Canadian coast south to North Carolina and west to the Ohio River valley. Two types of homes reflected the forested environment of this region. Wickiups (or wigwams) and longhouses were wood-framed structures covered with plants or bark. The inhabitants had **access** to rivers, lakes, and the Atlantic coastline.

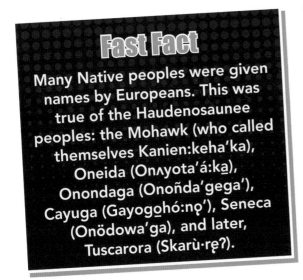

Fast Fact

Many Native peoples were given names by Europeans. This was true of the Haudenosaunee peoples: the Mohawk (who called themselves Kanien:keha'ka), Oneida (Onʌyota'á:ka), Onondaga (Onoñda'gega'), Cayuga (Gayogohó:nǫ'), Seneca (Onödowa'ga), and later, Tuscarora (Skarù·rę?).

Dugouts—boats carved from logs—and birch-bark canoes provided transportation. Animals such as deer and turkey were sources of food and clothing. Maize (corn), beans, and squash were key crops.

Northeast peoples included the Pequot, Wampanoag, Ho-Chunk, Algonquin (who called themselves Omàmiwinini), Hurons (Wendat), Mohican (Muh-he-con-neok), Ojibwa (Anishinaabe), Mohegan (Mohiingan), and Fox (Meskwaki). Many spoke Iroquoian or Algonquian languages.

In some communities, the leader was called a sachem. The position was passed from father to son, or to a daughter if no son was available. Sachems conducted business with other groups, acted as judges,

The Haudenosaunee, also called the Iroquois, of the Northeast united to make decisions in order to live in peace. *Haudenosaunee* means "People of the Longhouse." They lived in structures like this.

FIRST AMERICANS

The story of America goes back further than the 1492 arrival of Christopher Columbus. People came to North America as early as 30,000 years ago. These were the ancestors of the Native Americans present when Europeans first came to America. They crossed a land bridge that existed then between northwestern North America and northeastern Asia. The expanse stretched 1,000 miles (1,609 kilometers). It may have lasted about 14,000 years. Some people chose to stay north, while others ventured south. Eventually, many peoples began to settle and practice agriculture.

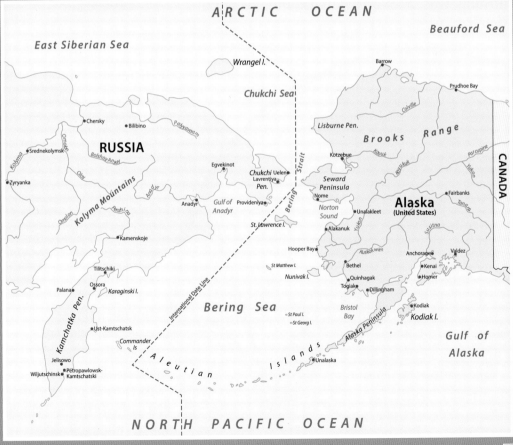

The Bering Strait now separates Asia and North America.

and assigned hunting grounds. They had assistants who were sometimes chosen by the group's senior women.

Southeast Cultures

Native Americans of the Southeast lived from what is now North Carolina south to the Gulf of Mexico and west to the Mississippi River. With a warm climate and long growing season, farming was a major part of life. A huge plateau—an area of high, level ground—between the Appalachian Mountains and the Atlantic coast was the most fertile region—and the most populated. Hunting for large game such as bear took place in the fall to provide meat and clothing in colder weather. Fish were plentiful year-round for coastal peoples.

Some well-known Southeast peoples

About 4,000 Cherokee died as they were forced to settle west. This event was called the Trail of Tears. The Eastern Band of Cherokee managed to escape authorities to stay in the east.

Choctaw villages sometimes played stickball games to resolve differences. This is an 1834 painting of a skilled stickball player named Tullockchishko.

Fast Fact

Southeast peoples spoke different languages, mostly from the Muskogean family of languages. However, some spoke a Siouan language, and the Cherokee spoke an Iroquoian language.

were the Cherokee, Choctaw (Chahta), Chickasaw (Chikasha), Creek (Muscogee), Seminoles, Natchez, Caddo, and Apalachee. Homes could be quite different but included wickiups and earthen dwellings. Later, chickees—houses on stilts with thatched roofs and no walls—were ideal for the swampy, hot land of Florida's Seminoles. Many Southeast peoples were forced to leave their lands by the Indian Removal Act of 1830.

A Cherokee man named Sequoyah created a writing system of 86 symbols for the Cherokee language.

Some Plains peoples chased bison over small cliffs as a hunting method, as this mid-19th century painting shows.

WEST OF THE MISSISSIPPI

Many Native Americans located in the middle of the continent lived in places less suited to agriculture. Nevertheless, they created successful societies thanks to their knowledge of and appreciation for the natural resources of their varied environments.

Plains Cultures

From today's Canada south to Texas and from the Rocky Mountains east to the Mississippi River lie the North American plains, largely dry and windy with few trees. The Indigenous peoples of the Plains—including the Hidatsa, Omaha, Pawnee, Arikara, Mandan (Numakiki), and Crow (Apsáalooke)—relied on one animal: bison. Bison, sometimes mistakenly called buffalo, provided meat, fur, fuel, and bones. Hunting expeditions could last weeks but fed and clothed a family for a whole year. It took many people to complete a successful hunt.

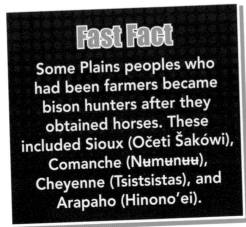

Fast Fact

Some Plains peoples who had been farmers became bison hunters after they obtained horses. These included Sioux (Očeti Šakówi), Comanche (Numunuu), Cheyenne (Tsistsistas), and Arapaho (Hinono'ei).

Grassy plains and river valleys to the east were centers of Plains agriculture. Indigenous peoples there created earth-lodge villages. Later, tepees of bison skin became the transportable homes of hunters.

Before Europeans introduced horses to the Americas, some Plains peoples disguised themselves as animals to get close to bison on their hunts.

Southwest Cultures

Native Americans of the Southwest inhabited mesas, canyons, deserts, and mountains. This area includes modern-day southern Utah and Colorado, Arizona, New Mexico, and Mexico. Little rain, a hot climate,

Black Coal, shown here, was a leader of a Northern Arapaho band in the late 1800s.

Hogans like this were traditional shelters for the Navajo (Diné) people.

and rocky terrain seem an unlikely combination for prosperous cultures, but early communities survived by gathering seeds, roots, and cactus fruits. They lived in caves. Later, the Colorado River and Rio Grande created opportunities for growing crops, such as corn, beans, squash, and cotton. Birds, snakes, deer, and jackrabbits were other sources of food.

Southwest groups included the Pueblo (such as the Zuni and Hopi), Navajo (Diné), Apache, Quechan (Yuma), Pimas (Akimel O'odham), and Tohono O'odham. The Pueblo peoples built apartment-like homes of adobe and stone. The Pimas near the Gila River built houses of adobe mud, cactus, and willow.

NORTHERN PEOPLES

The Subarctic peoples lived north of the Plains peoples. They moved in small bands but sometimes came together. Subarctic peoples—including Innu (Montagnais and Naskapi), Cree (Nêhiyawak), Chipewyan, Gwich'in, Tanaina, and Deg Xinag (Ingalik)—fished, hunted, and gathered foods. They lived in homes that were built half-underground to protect them from the cold.

The people of the Arctic region lived even farther north, in today's northern Canada and Alaska. They included the Inuit, Iñupiat, Yupik (Yupiit), and Aleut. They survived in small groups of families in very cold temperatures, hunting, gathering, and fishing. In winter, some built snow homes called *iglu* or *igluvigaq* (igloo). Houses of wood and earth provided more permanent homes, however.

Great Basin Cultures

The Great Basin in western North America is named for its bowl-like landscape and is surrounded by the mountains of the Sierra Nevada in the west and the Wasatch Range of the Rockies in the east. This area includes today's states of Utah and Nevada as well as parts of Oregon, Idaho, Wyoming, Colorado, Arizona, Montana, and California. A large amount of the region's water—notably the Great Salt Lake—is salty, and much of the land is desert. Since agriculture was difficult, most peoples relied on hunting and gathering. Seeds, roots, pine nuts, and small game such as rabbits and snakes were part of the Great Basin diet. Northern

Fast Fact

Some Great Basin groups, such as the Shoshones (Newe/Neme), lived near water and could fish and hunt waterbirds.

A Paiute man sleeps in a wickiup in the late 1800s.

and eastern peoples in this region adopted horses and bison hunting after the Spanish arrived.

The Great Basin was home to the Washoe (Wá·šiw), Mono (Nim), Paiute (Numu), Bannock (Nimi), Ute (Núuchi-u), and Gosiute (Goshute) peoples. Housing included wickiups, brush shelters, and later, tepees. As hunters and gatherers, small family groups moved when necessary. People only followed the leaders of these bands as long as the band was successful in providing food for its members and in waging war. If people lost faith in their leader, they would join another leader's band or create a new band.

A Hupa, or Hoopa, man fishes in this 1923 photograph by Edward Curtis.

Peoples on the western side of the continent were just as varied as in other cultural areas. Each group's ways of life were **unique**, matched to the available natural resources and landscape.

California Cultures

The peoples of modern-day California and Baja California (Mexico) enjoyed wide-ranging landscapes. The Pacific coast, the Sierra Nevada mountain range, plateaus, basins, wetlands, and even deserts offered food sources. Major groups included the Hupa, or Hoopa, (Na:tinixwe); Yurok (Oohl); Pomo; Yuki; Wintun (Wintu); Maidu; and Chumash.

Fast Fact

There were about 20 different language groups spoken in the California region, and each of these groups included many languages.

Many California Indigenous peoples lived in groups of a few hundred to a few thousand. Farming occurred only along the Colorado River. Gathering was the easiest way to find food for most, and acorns were perhaps the most important food source. Fishing and hunting were also essential. Housing varied from round, wood-framed, single-family dwellings to multifamily, apartment-like buildings. Dugouts and

The Chumash have been making *tomol* boats for at least 1,500 years.

reed rafts were used for fishing and transportation. The Chumash people of Southern California made large ocean-going boats of redwood planks and **asphalt**.

Northwest Cultures

The Native Americans of the Northwest occupied the Pacific coast from what is now northern California to Alaska. This is a region of mountains and **temperate** rain forests. Fish, birds, sea mammals, and wild plants were abundant, so agriculture was largely unneeded. Villages were built near water, and large, rectangular homes had removable walls and roofs. Villages were organized into groups called "houses," which could have more than 100 people. Northwest groups include the Tlingit, Haida, Tsimshian, Coast Salish, Kwakiutl, Nuu-chah-nulth (Nootka), and Chinook.

Communities often had ranks, from the chief to enslaved captives and everyone else between.

Fast Fact

The widow of a chief could become the leader of a house group.

TOTEM POLES

Northwest Coast Indigenous art is famous for stone and wood carvings, seaworthy boats, and intricate baskets. Totem poles were

not a traditional part of their culture, although Northwest groups are now well known for them. Totem poles became common when Native Americans began trading with Europeans. The poles are not religious objects. They are created for several reasons, including to display the crests of their owner, to remember a loved one's life, to mark a grave, and even to shame someone who has done something wrong. Totem poles also reflect a person's wealth.

Every image on a totem pole has a meaning, but the meaning is only completely known to the owners and the artists.

Salmon were an important source of food for both the Northwest and Plateau peoples. They used clever methods of fishing, such as placing white stones on the river bottom to help them better spot the salmon.

Ceremonial events called potlatches marked some Northwest cultures. The host of the potlatch showed wealth by giving gifts to guests. A potlatch could elevate the rank of the host.

Anotklosh, a leader of the Taku Tlingit, wore a Chilkat woven robe that reflected his high rank.

Plateau Cultures

Plateau Indigenous peoples inhabited lands east of the Northwest Coast peoples. These include today's northern Idaho and Montana, eastern Oregon, eastern Washington, and southern British Columbia, Canada. The climate was temperate and usually mild. Mountains kept rain from hitting lower elevations. Grasslands and deserts were the main setting for hunting and gathering, with permanent settlements located by rivers. In

This Nez Percé (Niimíipuu) man was painted by artist George Catlin around 1832.

the summer, they used small, cone-shaped houses for each family. Larger A-frame homes, some up to 150 feet (45.7 meters) long, were used in the winter by more than one family. With the arrival of Spanish horses, some Plateau people became bison hunters.

Among the many Plateau groups were the Modoc (Maklak), Nez Percé (Niimíipuu), Yakama (Waptailmim), Kutenai (Kootenai), Spokan (Spokane), Coeur d'Alene (Schitsu'ums), Walla Walla (Walúulapam), and Umatilla (Imatalamɫáma).

Much of the art showing Christopher Columbus arriving in the Americas suggests Europeans as heroic and Native Americans as primitive. Recent artists are correcting this imagery.

A NEW WORLD BEGINS

The arrival of Christopher Columbus in the Americas in 1492 was a turning point for Native Americans. The Spanish began establishing settlements in the Southeast in the late 1500s. The British, Dutch, French, and other Europeans followed. Interactions between the Europeans and Native Americans varied, sometimes violent and sometimes peaceful. No matter Europeans' intentions, their arrival had deadly **repercussions** for Indigenous peoples.

Jamestown

In many instances, the initial relationship between Native Americans and Europeans was friendly. At Jamestown in Virginia, the first permanent British settlement in North America, the colony's first years were marked with hunger and sickness. The nearby Powhatan provided meat and corn in exchange for European tools, clothes, and other goods.

Fast Fact

Jamestown was nearly abandoned. John Rolfe's planting of West Indian tobacco saved it, but tobacco farming also led to enslaved Africans being brought to the settlement to work in the fields.

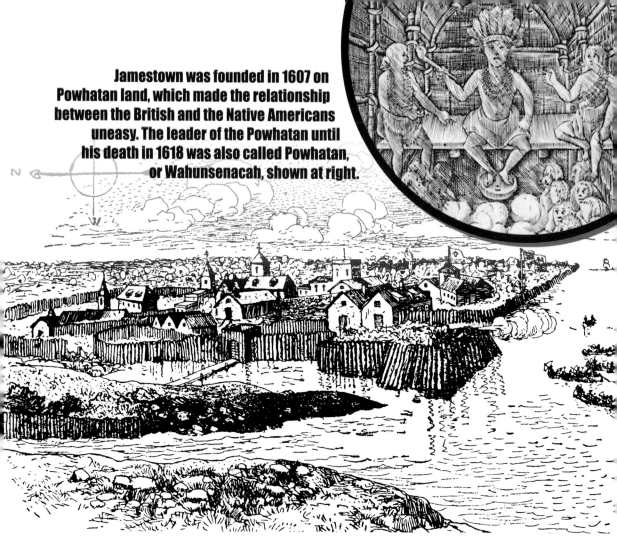

Jamestown was founded in 1607 on Powhatan land, which made the relationship between the British and the Native Americans uneasy. The leader of the Powhatan until his death in 1618 was also called Powhatan, or Wahunsenacah, shown at right.

However, after a **drought** and thievery by the British, the Powhatan stopped trading food to the British, resulting in near starvation in Jamestown. Hostilities ended for a time when colonist John Rolfe married the Powhatan leader's daughter, Amonute (also called Pocahontas).

Conflicts Increase

As the number of colonists swelled, a series of conflicts occurred in the Northeast. The Pequot War began in 1636 between the British and the

FARMING: A LIFESAVING SKILL

The Wampanoag taught settlers called Pilgrims, who came to New England on the *Mayflower* in 1620, how to plant crops. Climbing plants, such as beans, were planted next to tall plants, such as cornstalks. Growing beans alongside corn was beneficial to the corn. Corn (and most other crops) drain nitrogen—an element necessary for plant growth—from the soil. Beans, however, put nitrogen back into the soil. Another Native American farming method included burning the previous year's leftover crops. The ash made the soil more fertile for new plants. In 1621, the Wampanoag and the Pilgrims shared a harvest feast we now remember as the first Thanksgiving.

Fast Fact

In 1680, the Pueblo of the Southwest **revolted** against the Spanish and remained independent for 12 years. This was the only successful Indigenous revolt against European powers in North America.

Pequot people who lived along the Connecticut River. Later, some Native peoples started King Philip's War (1675–1676) to take a stand against the white settlement of Native lands, but it ended with the destruction of many Wampanoag villages.

To the south, Spanish **conquistador** Hernando de Soto swept through the Southeast in the mid-1500s. Beginning in Florida in 1539, he enslaved many Native Americans as he headed north.

After the Pequot War, the British claimed all Pequot territory. Surviving Pequot were forced to flee or be killed or enslaved.

The Natchez had little contact with Europeans until the late 1600s. However, wars with the French in the early 1700s resulted in the near **eradication** of this group.

Deadly Diseases

The biggest killer of Native Americans during European settlement was disease. The Europeans had lived with certain diseases for thousands of years and had developed some **immunity** to illnesses such as influenza, smallpox, measles, and cholera. Native Americans had no immunity to these, and diseases spread quickly, even reaching farther inland than the Europeans had traveled. The elderly, the keepers of oral histories and stories, were often the first to die, a blow to the traditions of many cultures. Perhaps 90 percent of all Native Americans died of diseases carried by Europeans.

Moving West

The British Proclamation of 1763 named the area between the Appalachian Mountains and the Mississippi River "Indian Territory." However, European settlers continued to move west. After the United States was founded, it established a pattern of forcing Native Americans to new lands and then taking over those lands. **Reservations** were created for some Indigenous groups, but certain parts of Native cultures would not survive for future generations.

Reservations meant that Native Americans had to change their ways of life. Some had to give up hunting. Many were made to give up their language, clothing, and religion too.

Many Native American groups hope to revive parts of their culture for new generations.

A TIMELINE OF INDIGENOUS AMERICA

around 28,000 BCE	People begin to arrive in North America.
around 14,000 BCE	The land bridge connecting North America and Asia begins to close.
around 2000 BCE	Native Americans in the Southwest grow corn.
500 CE	The Chumash build ocean-going boats.
1492	Christopher Columbus arrives in the Caribbean.
1607	The first permanent British settlement is established at Jamestown, aided at first by Powhatan people.
1636	The Pequot War begins.
1675	King Philip's War begins.
1680	The Pueblo win their revolt against the Spanish.
1731	The French nearly destroy the Natchez people.
1763	A British proclamation names the area between the Appalachian Mountains and the Mississippi River "Indian Territory."
1821	Sequoyah completes the Cherokee writing system.
1830	The Indian Removal Act forces Native Americans to territory west of the Mississippi River.
1851	The Indian Appropriations Act creates the reservation system.

1. What are the advantages or disadvantages of learning about Native Americans by grouping them into cultural areas?

2. What are some challenges to learning about the past of different Native American groups?

3. Why do you think some Indigenous peoples changed their way of life when horses were brought to North America?

4. Why do you think some Native American groups helped European settlers, while others were hostile to them?

access: The ability to use or enter something.

asphalt: A brownish-black substance found in nature that hardens when it cools.

conquistador: A Spanish conqueror or adventurer.

cultural: Having to do with the beliefs and ways of life of a group of people.

drought: A long period of weather so dry that crops cannot grow.

eradication: The act of destroying something completely.

immunity: A body's ability to resist disease.

Indigenous: Having to do with the first peoples of an area.

repercussion: Something, often bad, that happens as a result of an action that affects people for a long time.

reservation: Land set aside by the U.S. government for Native Americans to live on.

revolt: To turn against an established authority. Also, an uprising against an established authority.

temperate: Describing a climate with temperatures that are not very hot or very cold.

unique: One of a kind.

Books

Beason, Jimmy. *Native Americans in History: A History Book for Kids*. Emeryville, CA: Rockridge Press, 2021.

Louis, David Levering. *Native Americans and European Settlers*. New York, NY: PowerKids Press, 2020.

Sorell, Traci. *We Are Still Here! Native American Truths Everyone Should Know*. Watertown, MA: Charlesbridge, 2021.

Websites

Native American
www.loc.gov/classroom-materials/immigration/native-american/
The Library of Congress presents links to learn about Native American history in the 19th and 20th centuries.

Native Voices
www.nlm.nih.gov/nativevoices/timeline/index.html
Read a detailed timeline of events related to Native American history.

Trail of Tears
cherokeehistorical.org/trail-of-tears/
Learn about the Trail of Tears from the Cherokee Historical Association.